Ace Your Air Force Academy Interview

by Lauren Elliott

Table of Contents

Chapter 1
INTRODUCTION

You have decided to go to the United States Air Force Academy. Congratulations! The hard work BEGINS with the application process and will continue until you graduate. Attending a Service Academy is unlike anything you have ever done before. It will test you beyond your limits, and I promise at some point in time you WILL want to go home. That being said, I am very proud and happy to have graduated from the Air Force Academy and wish anyone the same amazing experience if that is their goal.

This book is focused on helping you with the interview portion of the application process. I worked in the Air Force Academy Admissions office and have evaluated thousands upon thousands of students for acceptance at the Air Force Academy. This book is based on that experience, and I believe the information contained within these pages can really improve your interview skills. If you would like additional help during any part of the application process or want help with mock interviews please visit us at www.academypros.com. The Professional Service Academy Consultants would be happy to help you! Also visit the Lauren Elliott Author Page on Amazon for additional titles.

If you recently decided to go to the Air Force Academy you may feel at a disadvantage to those who have been preparing for a Service Academy before high school. As a senior in high school there is very little you can do to change your grades or add addition activities to your resume. BUT the interview is something you can prepare for and absolutely amaze those interviewing you. For the Air Force Academy you will have an interview with your Admissions Liaison Officer and an interview with your Congressman and/or Senator. Some Congressmen and Senators do not have interviews, but most do. The interviews are conducted by a panel of people usually representing all of the Service Academies. Also, you might be interested in ROTC and ROTC scholarships. This process requires an interview as well. This book will help with ALL of the interviews. In fact, this book will teach you an easy to learn interview style that can be used during any type of interview (other college interviews, internship interviews, job interviews, etc.) you will have throughout your entire life. So, keep this book and re-read it when an interview is coming up.

Chapter 2
WARNING

I will give you fair warning. Just reading this book WILL NOT help you have a great interview. You MUST be willing to put the work in and apply the techniques. This is not a long book, but there are exercises in this book with suggestions on what and how many to do. DO THEM. Interviewing is a skill and like any skill it must be learned and then PRACTICED until it becomes natural and an integrated part of your skillset. I have taught many students these skills and only with practice have they improved. I promise if you learn the techniques I teach and work to apply them, your interview skills will improve dramatically. You can and will shine during any interview. You will feel prepared and wonder why anyone feels that interviews are difficult.

Consider this line of thinking. If you want to go to a Service Academy, you get good grades and take Honors Courses, AP/IB Courses, or other Advanced Courses. So, let me ask a question. Would you ever go into your Calculus class on test day without learning the material, taking notes, or reviewing any of the teacher's examples? Would you go in blind and hope for an A? No, you would not. That would be stupid, right? You take notes in class, do your homework, and at least the night before the test review your homework and notes. Interviews are the same as a Calculus test, it is not something you just "know" how to do. You have to put in the work, practice (do your homework) and review right before the big day. So, put in the work and dazzle those interviewing you!

Chapter 3
PUT YOURSELF IN THE SHOES OF YOUR INTERVIEWER

The purpose of an interview is to see who you really are. A person cannot be reduced to a transcript, resume, and an essay or two. People are far more interesting and complex than that. The interview is a chance for the interviewer to see beyond your academic scores and beyond the list of activities on a piece of paper. You need to come alive to them. You need to be a three-dimensional person with interesting stories and human depth. If done correctly, the interview is a chance for you to stand out from the crowd.

An interview is a very effective tool for people to decide who the best of the best is, and who really stands head and shoulders above the rest. The interview is considered an excellent discriminator. Now, put yourself in the shoes of the interviewers. They are trying to pick who should attend the Academy from a list of students. Those interviewing have all the resumes, essays and transcripts. Everybody has high a GPA. Everyone has high SAT scores and ACT scores. Everyone has a huge list of activities. Over half are Captain of some sports team. The other half is on the short list for valedictorian. Some are sports team Captains and valedictorian. The completion is fierce.

Now, you are probably the best, and/or are valedictorian in your school. You are the smartest, the fastest, the brightest, and everyone in your town knows it. But the interviewers are looking at the best of every high school and the best in every community. Unfortunately, "the best" looks very similar. You look like everyone else on paper. But you are NOT like everyone else. You are unique, interesting, and most of all you REALLY want to go to the Air Force Academy. So, how can you stand out? The interview! It is the tool used to make the deciding choice so you need to impress the interviewer.

In any interview think about the person interviewing you and what they want to see. In the case of Service Academy and ROTC interviews, they are interested in three main categories leadership, character, and participation in a variety of school sports, activities, and community involvement.

Leadership: They want to see examples that depict your problem solving skills, ability to take and give direction, and ability to work with a variety of people.

Character: They want to see examples of integrity. Examples that show you have solid integrity under pressure and that you exhibit integrity at all times.

Participation in a variety of activities: They want to see examples that you participate in a variety of school activities like sports, clubs, choir, band, and school leadership. Also, they will look for examples of community involvement, such as church, volunteer work, community activities, demonstrated leadership activities in your community, recreational sports, and work experience. They do not expect for you to have participated in all the listed activities (and there are many more examples listed), instead they are looking to see you have participated in a variety of things from each of these categories. Variety is the key word. Not just sports, not just school clubs, and not just volunteer work.

Did you notice anything similar across those three categories? EXAMPLES. Yes they want to see examples. There is a catch though. Remember to see your interview through the eyes of the panel. The interviewer has your resume. If you offer your examples as a huge list, you are not adding anything they did not already know about you. Examples in an interview are stories or antidotes about you and your involvement in leadership, character, and activities.

They want to know about you. They want to know details that make you different from everybody else. Example stories give you life and give you a third dimension that other students will not have. They want to be able to decide if you are someone who will be able to handle the challenging environment of the United States Air Force Academy. It is stressful. It is physically exhausting and academically demanding. They need to know whomever they pick will be able to handle those stresses. They are trying to determine if you will be able to organize your time and juggle multiple activities. They want to know that when you are under stress you will continue to have excellent character. Also, if you have the potential to be a great leader. You need to think from that point of view as you create your examples. The interviewer will determine what type of person you are based on your past performance. The better and more detailed your stories, the better they can predict your future success.

To do this you need to brag about yourself through your example stories. But flat out bragging can come across as rude or hard to listen to. You probably know someone that you hate to be around because all they do is talk about how wonderful they are. There is a fine line between bragging and showing those interviewing you that you will succeed at the Academy. Here is the essence of annoying bragging, "I can do this and this and this….." No examples and no engaging story. But there is an acceptable way to brag. The method is called STAR stories. A STAR story offers a way to brag about yourself that sounds very acceptable to people because it comes across as interesting and engages people through the story. Very succinctly, you tell people what you have accomplished in your life and offer results from your actions. The panel can then judge for themselves, from your actions and results, if what you accomplished was amazing or not. The STAR story method helps you tell them about yourself in a manner that comes across as very factual and very interesting. You are not bragging at that point of time. You are telling them about yourself and it really excites a panel to hear about students doing amazing things.

Chapter 4
STAR STORIES

STAR stories are a very simple yet effective interview method. I promise you that if you put in the work to craft excellent STAR stories that your interviews will stand head and shoulders above everyone else's interview.

STAR

S: Situation

T: Task

A: Action

R: Result or Results

This method is an extremely effective way to frame the experiences in your life and to tell interviewers about your life and your experiences. Each part of the STAR acronym is important, but the last two (your actions, your results) are probably the most important and where you should spend the most time explaining. I want to highlight one other item. This is a STAR story not a STAR list. You want to create a story, create something memorable. Most students and actually most adults when asked any question about themselves start to list a bunch of qualities. This is not very interesting or does it tell the interviewer anything new. You need to create a story that shows the interviewer what type of person you are.

So, how do you create a STAR story? Take events in your life where you have accomplished something, lead an activity, helped someone, saw someone compromising their integrity, got through a difficult time in your life, solved a challenging problem, or confronted a teacher or coach on an issue that meant a lot to you. There is a brainstorming exercise later, but let's start by thinking about a time you lead an event or a group of people. It does not matter if you were the formal leader or if it was in school, sports, or in the community. Got an event in mind? Start with the S, write down a few thoughts and repeat for each letter of STAR.

Here are a few examples.

Example 1

The Junior Class organizes prom (Situation) and I was in charge of decorations (Task). I recruited a committee of other students and a teacher as a supervisor. I made sure to create an agenda and we met weekly. At our meetings, I encouraged participation from the group and assigned each member tasks. At the meetings we shared our progress and helped each other with anything not completed. I made sure to update our teacher of our progress and discussed what she could do to help us (Action). As a result of our organization and work together attitude the prom decorations were the best our school had seen and had come $100 under budget (Results).

Comments: The situation and task were kept short and gave just enough information to give the listener context. The list of actions accomplished was specific to what the speaker actually did. If the speaker had simply stated "I organized the committee to get the decorations done" the listener would not have any true detail to what the speaker had done. Notice the verbs used; recruited, created, encouraged, shared, discussed, updated. Verbs tell actions. Use verbs to describe the actions. The results were clear; saved $100 and best decorations seen.

Example 2

I was the Co-Chair on my church's youth committee. Our committee was in charge of organizing and executing all activities for the Youth Adventure Weekend. A 3-night 4-day campout for over 300 youth (Situation). As Co-Chair, I needed to provide an overarching theme, create sub-committees, and insure everything was done (Task). I knew I wanted the event to be very special, so I spent days gathering information on what other groups had done from across the country. I gathered what I thought where the best activities. My theme was "The Lord will lead the way". I created a presentation that laid out all the activities and skits that would introduce each activity. I discussed with my Co-Chair who was thrilled I had a plan. We both presented the information to the rest of the youth committee and gained support from all. Everyone commented and the Youth Adventure Weekend was tweaked so all were excited. I assigned tasks, created sub-committees, and followed up on each (Action). The day of the event came and we were all prepared. I was thrilled when the adult leadership commented on how proud they were of me, my committee, and how well the event turned out (Results).

Comments: The situation and task were longer in this example but the speaker tried to give enough information so the listener could follow. Also, the length of the event and the numbers of youth were mentioned so the listener could understand the size of event planned. An event for 10 people is much different than a several day, overnight event for 300. The actions section contained several verbs to describe all that happened. The results discussed included that everything was prepared and ready for the event. Also, the results include comments that the adults were very happy with the speaker and the committee for the positive results.

Example 3

I was watching the news with my parents and saw that a tornado had completely destroyed a small town in Oklahoma. The screen showed a tiny girl holding her mom and crying.

The family had nothing, and I felt that I had to do something to help (Situation). The picture of the little girl really spoke to me. I decided that I would help the kids in the town by collecting teddy bears to make them feel better (Task). I started by asking my parents for help. They agreed to ask around at work for teddy bears and donations. Next, I called my church and asked to put in an announcement in the bulletin that Sunday to ask for donations. Last, I went to school and spoke with our Service League and asked how they could help. They offered to support a Teddy Bear Drive one Saturday at the local Mall. My parents and I collected the money and bears as they came in (Action). Before, I knew it our garage was filled with just over 2,000 teddy bears. With the help of the monetary donations and a few corporate sponsors we were able to ship all the bears to the town in Oklahoma. I will always treasure the thank you note and photo that came back showing kids with the bears (Results).

Comments: This is an excellent example of leadership. The speaker was not called as a formal leader for school or the community, instead she saw a need and formed a plan to fill the need. The actions clearly showed how the student rallied the community to help and it resulted in 2,000 teddy bears to kids in need. Remember you do not need to actually be a leader or a captain of a team to show leadership. You just need to step up and lead.

Example 4

I spent my summers mowing lawns in my neighborhood for extra spending money. One day an older gentleman, Mr. Smith, told that he was unable to pay me anymore and that I didn't need to mow his lawn again. About two weeks later, I was mowing across the street, and noticed Mr. Smith struggling to get his mower started (Situation/Task). I liked him and wanted to help him out. I knew he would have trouble pushing his old mower, even if he got it started. I told Mr. Smith to put his mower away, and I would handle the lawn. He protested. I explained that I would be happy to mow the lawn for free. I came back each week and mowed Mr. Smith's lawn. He couldn't pay me, but he would always bring me a root beer or lemonade (Action). At the end of the summer, Mr. Smith came by our house and spoke with my parents. He told them I had been mowing his lawn for free and that they had a wonderful son who they should be very proud of. I was embarrassed, but my parents were proud that I had helped Mr. Smith. I learned that service means a great deal to the people we help (Results).

Comments: In this example the Situation and Task were combined. The speaker's actions were very clear. He decided to help his neighbor by mowing the lawn even though he was not going to get paid. The results were a simple thank you and the speaker stated what he learned about service. This is an excellent STAR story about character. It is easy for someone to say they have good character, but this example SHOWS good character. If asked about your community service or your character, think about a time you have served someone and tell the story. It does not have to be a major event. It can be something small that you noticed and just decided to help. Your actions will give those interviewing you a very clear picture of what kind of person you are.

Example 5

I work at a sandwich shop a few evenings a week and on weekend. My job is to make the sandwiches and clean the tables. One evening, the night manager and I were cleaning up and getting ready to go home. I noticed that he took some of the money from the cash register out and separated it from the rest before he brought the drawer back to the safe in the back. This seemed odd, but I wasn't sure if he had to count it a special way or needed it separate for some reason. A few nights later, I saw him take the small amount he had separated and slip it into his pocket before heading back (Situation/Task). I knew that this wasn't right. I decided to talk to the owner of the shop. I came in early the next day to talk to him. I told him what I saw and kept to the facts without accusing the night manager of anything. I felt that the owner should look into it (Action). A few weeks later, I had a new night manager. The owner came in that evening and thanked me for speaking up about what I saw. Apparently, the old manager had been stealing small amounts for a while. Without my input, the owner would have never caught him (Results).

Comments: In this example the student demonstrates his integrity. He stated what he saw and that he knew he should speak to the owner. This resulted in the owner finding out that someone was stealing from the cash register. Have you ever seen something that you knew didn't seem right? Did you tell someone? If so then you have an excellent STAR story about integrity. Even if you didn't tell anyone you can still use it as a good STAR story. Think back to the event. What did you learn? What would you do now? If you had to do it over, would you tell someone? Why? The answers to these questions could be your result. Example: You saw someone cheating, but you didn't tell the teacher. To this day you still feel bad about not saying anything even though the event happened two years ago. You know now that you would say something because your conscience won't let another cheating incident like that go by without saying something. Show that you have learned and that you will do the right thing the next time.

Each example contained a story with the pertinent details. Details were specific to the situation and what was accomplished. You want to add color and life to your stories. If you have taken a writing course you will know that writing involves details. It is not just a tissue, it is a Kleenex. If talking about a car, it is not just a car. It is a Ford Mustang. You want the story to be succinct and no more than about a few minutes. To do that need you need to offer vivid details that create a picture. Take the example of the car from above. If I said that I drove a car, what do you picture? Some vague car shaped object or maybe your favorite car. Each person in the interview panel might picture something different. If I said I drove a red Ford Mustang everyone has pretty much the same picture in their head.

Adding specific, vivid details help everyone on the interview panel see the same picture. The trick is to decide what details are really important to the story. Too much detail can make a story drag on too long. In Example 2 the speaker included the detail about 300 youth attending the event. This definitely gives you a picture of how large the event was so it was an important detail. The detail stating the theme probably is not very important and could be left out. It is short though and adds some detail, but if a shorter answer is needed it could be left out. Look at the details of your story and make sure each offers substance to the story.

An important item to discuss about STAR stories is the results. Numbers, dollar figures, time saved or number of people led are very important to state in each STAR story. In fact, results are probably the most important part. Students usually leave out results whenever they are asked about their actions or activities. If you want to differentiate yourself from the other candidates adding the results of your actions will set you apart. In the above examples the results discussed were about dollars being saved, compliments from observers, number of teddy bears shipped, and lessons· learned. The more specific the results the better, but stating that an event went well with no problems IS a result and should be stated if that is all you can think of. If an event didn't go well state what you learned and how you would fix it the next time.

Brainstorming STAR stories

I have an activity for you to complete at the end of this section that will help brainstorm STAR stories. With it I want you to come up with eight or nine stories at least. If you could come up with more, great! But at least eight or nine. Also, you need to spend a dedicated amount of time writing them out. You need to physically write your STAR stories down. You do not have to write out every single detail or full sentences, but you do need to create a detailed outline for each story.

I suggest creating the following STAR stories.

- 3 positive leadership examples
- 1 negative leadership example (Include what you learned from the experience and how you would change your actions for the future.)
- 1 positive example about your character
- 1 negative example about your character or a negative example you have witnessed (If it was an example of your mistake include what you learned and how you would change your actions in the future. If you witnessed one of your friends or others lying, cheating or stealing include what you did and what did you learned from that experience.)
- 2-3 examples from school or community accomplishments

You need to vary the examples throughout your life. Do not pull every example from sports. Do not pull every example from junior ROTC. Provide examples from several of your activities. For example, one about junior ROTC, one about sports, one about leadership in your church, one about school involvement, one about academics, and one about a club. Pick examples from all over your life. Remember anytime that you use a negative example, or have any type of negative in the example, include what you learned and how you might improve if something similar happens. They are not looking for perfection in cadets. They want to know that you can learn from your mistakes and improve. Leadership is a skill that one continues to learn throughout their life. Mistakes happen, the important part is picking yourself up and improving upon yourself each day.

Brainstorming Activity

IMPORTANT: You must craft your STAR stories from this activity and practice them.

Below is a very comprehensive list of actions and activities. Many of them will probably not apply to you, but read through each one. The purpose of this activity is to get you thinking. Look at each word and ask yourself if you can think of ANY examples, unique stories, or thoughts you can associate with that word. If you think of something jot a note down or circle the word. As you go through the list you will notice that certain activities or stories will come up several times. Those ones are most likely good STAR stories. Once you have an idea of the stories you will write about look above at the recommended types of STAR stories. See if you can craft your stories towards those goals. If you come up with extra that is great, but make sure to come up with eight or nine in total.

LIST

Adapted (teaching styles/special tools)
Administered (programs)
Advised (people/peers/job-seekers)
Analyzed (data/blueprints/schematics/policies)
Appraised (services/value)
Arranged (meetings/events/training programs)
Assembled (automobiles/computers/apparatus)
Audited (financial records/accounts payable)
Budgeted (expenses)
Calculated (numerical data/annual costs/mileage)
Cataloged (art collection/technical publications)
Checked (accuracy/other's work)
Classified (documents/plants/animals)
Cleaned (houses/auto parts)
Coached (teams/students/athletes)
Collected (money/survey information/data/samples)
Compiled (statistics/survey data)
Confronted (people/difficult issues)
Constructed (buildings)
Consulted (on new designs/investment strategy)
Coordinated (events/work schedules)
Corresponded (with other departments/colleagues)
Counseled (students/peers/job-seekers)
Created (new programs/artwork/internet sites)
Cut (diamonds/concrete/fabric/glass/lumber)
Decided (which equipment to buy/priorities)
Delegated (authority)
Designed (data systems/greeting cards)
Directed (administrative staff/theatre productions)
Dispensed (medication/information)
Displayed (results/products/artifacts)
Distributed (products/mail)
Dramatized (ideas/problems/plays)
Edited (publications/video tape/)
Entertained (people)
Established (objectives/guidelines/policies)
Estimated (physical space/costs/staffing needs)

Evaluated (programs/instructors/peers/students)
Exhibited (plans/public displays/evidence)
Expressed (interest in development projects)
Facilitated (multimedia exhibit/conflict resolution)
Found (missing persons/appropriate housing)
Framed (houses/pictures)
Generated (interest/support)
Grew (plants/vegetables/flowers)
Handled (detailed work/data/complaints/toxins)
Hosted (panel discussions/foreign students)
Implemented (registration system/new programs)
Improved (maintenance schedule/systems)
Initiated (production/changes/improvements)
Inspected (physical objects/repairs/electrical work)
Installed (software/bathrooms/electrical systems/parts)
Interpreted (languages/new laws/schematics/codes)
Interviewed (people/new employees)
Invented (new ideas/machine parts)
Investigated (problems/violations/fraud)
Landscaped (gardens/public parks/indoor gardens)
Led (foreign tours/campus tours)
Listened (to others/to conference calls)
Located (missing information/facilities)
Maintained (transportation fleet/aircraft/diesel engines)
Managed (an organization/a mail room/a retail store)
Measured (boundaries/property lines/bridge clearance)
Mediated (between people/civil settlements)
Met (with dignitaries/public/community groups)
Monitored (progress of others/water flow/electric usage)
Motivated (workers/trainees)
Negotiated (contracts/sales/labor disputes)
Operated (equipment/hydraulic test stand/robotics equipment)
Organized (tasks/library books/data bases)
Painted (houses/cars/aircraft/interiors)
Patrolled (runways/public places/property/buildings)
Persuaded (others/customers)
Planned (agendas/international conferences)
Predicted (future needs/stock market trends)
Presented (major selling points/new products)

Prepared (reports/meals/presentations)
Printed (books/reports/posters)
Processed (human interactions)
Programmed (computers)
Promoted (events/new products/new technology)
Proofread (news/reports/training materials)
Protected (property/people)
Published (reports/books/software)
Purchased (equipment/supplies/services)
Questioned (people/survey participants/suspects/witnesses)
Raised (performance standards/capital investments)
Read (volumes of material/news releases)
Recorded (data/sales totals/music/video)
Recruited (people for hire/executives/Marines)
Rehabilitated (people/old buildings)
Repaired (mechanical devices/exhaust systems)
Reported (findings/monthly activity)
Researched (library documents/cancer/diseases)
Renewed (programs/contracts/insurance policies)
Reviewed (program objectives/books and movies)
Revised (instructional materials)
Scheduled (social events/doctor's appointments)
Sold (advertising space/real estate/cars)
Served (individuals)
Sewed (parachutes/clothing/upholstery)
Signed (for the hearing impaired)
Sketched (charts and diagrams)
Spoke (in public)
Supervised (others)
Taught (classes/math/science)
Tailored (clothing/services)
Televised (conferences/training/events/shows)
Tested (new designs/students/employees)
Updated (files)
Verified (reports/identity)
Volunteered (services/time)
Wrote (reports/training manuals)
Weighed (trucks/patients/precious metals)
Welded (bike frames/airframes/alloys)

X-rayed (limbs/stressed equipment)

Chapter 5
BASIC INTERVIEW TIPS

1) Confirm the time and place with your interviewer. Send any requested info on time or as early as possible.

2) Arrive ten to fifteen minutes early. Have a few minutes by yourself to be quiet and think about what you want to say. Stay away from others and focus on how you want to express yourself. Review your written STAR stories and review your resume. If you spent sufficient time on STAR stories you will already be well organized and they should encompass what is on your resume. It is in your best interest to formulate everything you can into a STAR story and PRACTICE them. The more you practice to a mirror, friends, or family, the more confident you will be. Take a deep breath before entering the room. Clear your mind from worries. You are ready!

3) Wear professional clothing. Guys, this includes a tie and khakis at least. Black slacks or a suit is fine too. You want to be clean shaven and wear nice shoes. Wear your best clothing. Ladies, black pants or a skirt, a nice top, minimal make-up, and well-groomed hair. Remember, you are not going to a club. You are not trying to look hot. You are trying to look professional. If you are confused you can ask an adult

who you think acts and looks professional their opinion on your wardrobe.

Note: If all you have is sneakers and you do not have a nice suit/dress, shoes, or something like that the Air Force Academy is not concerned with your bank account. They are concerned with the fact that you tried to dress properly. If the best thing you have is sneakers just try and clean them up, present a clean cut appearance. It is not about money. It is about preparation and thought. They want to know that you prepared appropriately. I would consider borrowing professional clothes from a friend or going to a thrift store. Do your very best, but if all you can afford/borrow is, a pair of khakis, and a polo shirt that is okay. Just make sure you are clean, presentable and act professionally. If you act professionally your personality will shine through and your clothing will not matter. Make the effort and show the interviewer that you want to attend the Air Force.

4) Eye contact. You must practice good eye contact during an interview. You do not want to stare intently though. In fact, if you are too intense it begins to feel awkward. You want to be able to look at those interviewing you most of the time, but you can look up, down or around as you speak. But you need to be conscious of your audience and look at them. With a one-one-one interview act like you are having a conversion with a

friend look them in the eye. In a group setting with a panel of people, several people will take turns asking you questions. Begin answering your question to the person who asked the question for about ten to fifteen seconds. Then, as you continue your answer start to look around the room and make eye contact with the rest of the people in the panel. Make them feel part of the conversation. Do not just focus on the one who asked you the question. All the people in the panel are evaluating you so they need to know that you are talking to all of them not just who asked the question. So, start with the person who asked the question and then look around the room at each person. Do not dart back and forth. Look at someone, make eye contact for a few seconds and then move on to the next person.   Always come back to who initially asked you the question to finish up.

5) Think about the question. When someone asks you a question you can think about it for a few seconds. Three or four seconds may seem like an eternity in your mind but do not panic. A few seconds to the interviewer is not going to look awkward. Just think for a few seconds, organize your thoughts, and then answer appropriately. If you have written and practiced your STAR stories it should be very simple to answer. Well written STAR stories can be slightly changed to accommodate the flavor of the question. Just filter through

which one make seems the most appropriate, adjust it slightly, and then start your answer.

But let's say you panic. You wrote your stories out, but you are drawing a blank on question number one. A ten to fifteen seconds pause will seem a little awkward. To give yourself a few more seconds to think you can clarify the question. That is an appropriate way to give yourself a little bit of time and not seem awkward when answering the question.

For example, question one is, "Tell me about yourself." Nothing comes to mind. You need to stall so you can clear your head and think. So you ask, "Are you more interested in my school or extracurricular activities?" Okay not the best respond to a question, but it will give you time to think. The interviewer answers, "school activities." Okay, school, you think. I can do school. "I am involved with track, cross country,....."

6) Add real excitement and emotion to your stories. Do not force emotion, but avoid sounding like your most boring teacher at school. Pay attention in class and see which teachers seem the most interesting. They probably are good at putting emotion and interest into their voices. Also, PRACTICE those STAR stories. I know I am foot stomping the STAR stories and there is a reason. The more you practice

them, the more confidence you will have as you talk and the more natural and engaging you will be to your audience. Additionally, you want to use your hands when you talk. Not too much but use your hands for emphasis. You do not want to seem stiff, very uncomfortable or very nervous. Keeping your hands glued to your lap will make you appear this way. The best way to help yourself is to practice with somebody. Practice with a friend, with your parents, with your stuffed animals, or a mirror. Other than the stuffed animals, you can get feedback if your speech and hand gestures seem natural.

7) Do not ramble or answer any question with a list. Example, if they ask, "What activities you are involved in?" A list may seem an appropriate way to answer and in a way it is. Offer three or four activities and then offer a short example or STAR story. Something like this, "I am Captain of my football team, I am vice President of the Senior Class, I play basketball, and I am involved in volunteering through my church. I really enjoy my volunteering activities. My favorite activity was cleaning a very nice older woman's home. Her husband had died and she had trouble keeping the house up so our church group had come to help her. I got talking with her while cleaning and offered to come back and mow her lawn. She had the biggest smile and it made me feel really good about helping her."

Now, if I had answered the question with a list of ten things what would the panel have learned about me? Nothing that my resume had not already told them. But the short story gave them a lot more about me than a list. Cleaning someone's house or mowing a lawn is not a major volunteer effort or even an amazing effort. But that little story will stick with the panel and they will remember. Lists are hard to remember, but stories last in our minds. Think about the little things you like or enjoy about your activities. I bet there is a story behind why you like or enjoy it.

8) Be short and concise. The STAR stories are (I can't emphasize STAR stories enough) going to help you in this tip. They help because you wrote them to be concise and you have practiced them. Follow the STAR story format to tell what is really important and you will stay on task.

9) Be real and avoid jokes. Humor is one of those things that is hard to judge. Some things are funny to some people and some things are not funny to others. Natural humor as you talk or tell a funny story that happened to you is okay but avoid outright jokes. They usually fall flat and could even offend someone. Be yourself and do not go out of your way to make people laugh.

10) Read your audience. The best way to do this is to practice and have confidence. If your audience looks a little glazed over or are looking sleepy, maybe you are going on too long. You could be rambling or could have given them a long list of things that they could not process. Read your audience's reaction and adjust. Think about your answers and think about the previous interview tips. Make adjustments and reengage with your panel. This is a fairly advanced tip and hard to accomplish, but can be done if you practice.

11) Know something about the Air Force and the Air Force Academy. Think of possible careers you might enjoy. There is no commitment to any certain career, but be prepared to tell the interviewer what kind of career would interest you. Also, you would be surprised how many students do not know anything about the Air Force or Air Force Academy itself. This is a huge, huge red flag for those interviewing you. You want to go to the Air Force Academy but have no idea about anything that the Air Force does or what the Air Force Academy is like. This is unacceptable in today's day and age. Get on the internet, read up on the websites, Facebook page and blogs, and watch some Air Force and Air Force Academy sponsored YouTube videos. It will take you thirty minutes to an hour. Well worth the time investment. You can ask your Admissions Liaison Officer questions about the Air Force and Air Force Academy. That is what he or she is there for. They

will appreciate the fact that you are interested. Also, you should try to find someone who went to the Air Force Academy to talk to. A friend of a friend or someone from your high school. Talk with them and ask what they thought the best and the hardest part about the Air Force Academy was for them.

LAST: I have said this over and over but it is probably the most important. Practice, practice, practice, practice! Here is the way I suggest to do this. Start with your STAR stories, write them out. Read them over and over again, memorize them, and then do a mock interview in front of a mirror. Ask family and friends to interview you and ask them for feedback. Really ask them for what you could have done better and what you can do to improve either your stories or presentation. When you interview with your parents or your friends, use your STAR stories to tell them something they may not even know about you. Try and tell them something new and interesting.

Chapter 6
BONUS: QUESTION BANK

Below is a list of possible questions that your Admission's Liaison Officer or the Congressional Panel may ask. The list is NOT all inclusive, but it is representative of the types of questions that will be asked. Read through the questions and come up with possible answers. Notice that the STAR stories you created will answer many of the questions listed below. The stories may need to be modified slightly, but the core of the story and results will be the same.

In what extracurricular activities did you participate in high school? What achievements did you obtain from these activities?

In your extracurricular activities, what prominent leadership roles did you have? Accomplishments?

Which of them give you the most satisfaction? Why?

What kind of periodicals do you read? What was the name of the last book you read not in connection with schoolwork?

Have you at any time directed/organized people or participated in efforts designed to fill a community need?

Are you in a leadership position in any of your activities?

Do you or have you ever had a part time job?

What is there about your job you like the most? Least?

How would your supervisor and co-worker describe you?

How would you characterize your friends?

What type of person do you most enjoy being with?

When and what has been the longest period of time you have been away from your parents?

Which physical sports are you involved in? What position?

What kind of physical exercise do you engage in on a regular basis?

Describe for me any work you've done with or for civic/charitable groups.

Tell me about a situation in which you helped someone handle a stressful or frustrating situation?

What do you feel are your outstanding qualities? In what areas of your life do you feel you can improve upon? Why?

Who motivates your actions the most, your parents or others? Or?

If you were given an order that you thought to be illegal or immoral, would you carry it out? What would you do?

Why should you receive an appointment?

What separates you from the crowd?

How would your friends describe you?

What are your best traits?

What is the single most difficult task you have had to accomplish that you did not want to do?

What community service do you do? Why?

Describe your best friend.

What's your best quality?

Who or what motivates you the most?

Tell me about a difficult experience that you have conquered. To what do you attribute this success?

Give me an example of when you had too much to do. How did you resolve the conflicts in your schedule? How did you establish priorities for your efforts?

Tell me about a situation in which you had to organize an activity?

If you could start your education over again, what would you change or do differently?

How do you manage and organize your time?

Do you feel you are capable of surviving the demanding physical and mental requirements of Air Force Academy life? Explain.

Describe a frustrating experience you faced and how you handled it.

Tell me about a time you had to explain how to do something to someone? What if they didn't understand your directions?

Describe a situation in which you has to lead a team/group in an activity. How well was the task carried out? Did you/they feel the directions were clear?

Define leadership.

Are you a good follower?

What is your best leadership example? Your worst?

Your hardest leadership experience?

Give examples of your effective leadership.

Describe a situation in which you strongly disagreed with a classmate, teacher, coach, or supervisor. How did you handle this situation?

Are you a "leader"? What experience have you had in leading other people?

Give three examples of effective leadership that you have displayed.

What extracurricular activities do you participate in at school? How involved are you in these activities?

What prominent leadership roles do/have you held in your extracurricular activities?"

What's your personal leadership style?

Describe a time you tried to lead, but failed? What did you learn?

Describe your worst stress situation.

Give examples of how you're a self-starter.

To whom do you look for good advice?

Why do you want to be an Air Force officer?

What is there about the Academy/ROTC do you think you may not like?

Describe the best argument someone could use to try and talk you out of becoming a military officer. How would you answer that?

Why do you want to attend a Military Academy instead of a regular college or university?

When and how did you first get interested?

How does your family feel about this?

Describe your typical daily schedule now.

Which parent or other adult has the most influence on you?

Any relatives or friends of the family ever attend one of the academies? Any in the military?

What will you do if no Air Force Academy appointment is offered? Why?

What will be your major? Why?

What will be your career? Why?

How long do you think you'll remain in the military?

Are you interested in making the military your career? Why?

If you had to pay tuition at the Air Force Academy, would you still apply?

Do you have any career goals, either in or out of the military life?

What do you expect life at an Academy to be like?

How much physical activity are you accustomed to? Do you feel capable of competing physically with other cadets at the Air Force Academy?

Which are your favorite high school courses, and why?

What do you dislike most about school?

Who do you regard as the outstanding individual of this decade?

How do your parents feel about your attendance at the Air Force Academy?

Are your parents employed? Occupations? Where? (Location)

How many brothers and sisters do you have?

Which of your parents exercise the most influence over you?

Are any of your relatives or friends graduates of an Academy?

Have any of your relatives been a member of the Armed Forces?

If you are not awarded a nomination to the Air Force Academy, where do you hope to continue your education?

Do you plan on participating in the athletic program at the Air Force Academy, either interscholastic or intramural?

What do you think you will learn from a Military Academy that you could not learn from another university?

Do you have any heroes? Military, historical, star teacher

Who has had the biggest influence in your life?

If a younger student came to you and asked how to get where you are what would you tell them?

What is your opinion of the Honor Code?

The Honor Code, among other things, requires that you report all violations you have observed or have knowledge of—would you?

Can you live up to the Honor Code?

What do you think the state of our country is?

What did your parents tell you not to say?

What is your opinion of the Military Honor Code?

Define Integrity

The Air Force Academy honor code has become rather controversial. Do you agree that cadets who are found cheating, or who tolerate others who cheat, should be dismissed from the Academy?

In what subject do you do your best work?

Do you feel your grades indicate your true ability? Why?

Have you won or been awarded any scholastic honors?

Must you work hard for your math grades or do they come easily?

Are there any math or science courses you could have taken and didn't? Why?

Describe for me your perception of Basic Cadet Training to include the physical and mental challenges.

What was your best source of information on Basic Cadet Training?

Chapter 7
BONUS: WHY A SERVICE ACADEMY?

The Professional Service Academy Consultants at www.academypros.com believes that a student MUST know and understand why they want to attend the Air Force Academy. The why needs to be personal and be more introspective then "I've wanted to go there since I was seven." There are several reasons this is an important question for a student to answer. One, it is one of the questions asked in interviews with the nomination panels and the Admissions Liaison Officer. Also, in essay form, a nomination source and the Air Force Academy will want to know the answer. Two, a student's why will motivate them during hard times.

I am an Air Force Academy graduate and I have four daughters. I am amazingly grateful for the opportunity that the Air Force Academy gave me. But, it was an incredibly difficult and challenging experience. I am very grateful for that challenge, and there is no way I would force any of my four daughters to attend if they did not want to. If they wanted to go, I would support them in every manner possible. But, it has to be their decision, and I understand that, because it was very, very difficult for me to stay. After you get past the first year, it becomes much easier, and you can see the purpose behind the difficult first year. The first year is tough, and you really have to have a very powerful why to be able stay.

As a student considering a Service Academy, you must understand your why and not just on a cursory level. Sitting on the admissions panels and admissions boards, I read over a thousand answers to this question. Seventy-five percent of applicants would answer because I'm patriotic and I feel it is my duty. Many other applicants would answer, I've always wanted to be a pilot. The third most common response was, my parents have served in the military and I want to do so as well. None of those answers are wrong, or bad, but, they are very typical. And though you may feel any of these to be true, it is not very telling about your personality. Nor does it give the board, the panel, or whoever you are answering this question to, any real insight into you. You have very little opportunity to express yourself, to convey who you are as an individual, and show the admissions panel why you really deserve to be at the Air Force Academy. So you must have an excellent why.

There are twelve thousand applicants and only a little over a thousand spots. You may have great SATs, excellent grades, a million extra-curricular activities, and you may be the greatest kid in your hometown, but you are competing against the other greatest kids in their hometowns across America. To the panel or board, you seem like everyone else. You MUST differentiate yourself. Expressing an insightful and interesting why you want to go to the Air Force Academy is one way you can. Also, understanding your true "why" will help keep you going when times are really, really tough. I promise you, there will be days when you want to go home and feel staying is NOT worth it. But a well-defined why gives you that reason to stay.

How do you find your why? Find a quiet spot and do some thinking, why a Service Academy? Start with your basic reasons. Say your answer is, "because I feel a patriotic duty." That is fine, then ask yourself why again. Why do you feel it is you duty? Maybe your next answer is, my parents served in the military, and I feel that was a really great way to show patriotism. That is great too, but why? Go down another level or maybe two levels deeper.

I did this exercise for myself. I sat down and thought about my why. Why did I want to attend the Air Force Academy? My first answers were because I felt patriotic, I thought it was a huge challenge, I wanted to be a leader, and I wanted to do and be more. So why did I really want those things? I decided it was because of my father. My dad is my hero to this day. But WHY is he my hero? And I thought because he served in the military, he is a good person and he exemplifies to me all that I want and could be. What happened in my life that made Dad my hero? And I thought of a story.

When I was about five years old, I was at the grocery store with my Dad. I knew it was wrong to take anything from a store and my parents had told me not to take candy without paying for it. Then, I saw an opened box of candy with most of the candy spilled all over the floor. I thought, "Eating candy off the floor can't be stealing, right?" So, I took the candy off the floor, put it in my mouth, and started to eat. A few minutes later my Dad asked what I was eating. I told him candy that I had found on the floor. He grabbed the box, took my arm, and marched me up to customer service. By this time, I was confused and a little scared. He asked to see the store manager. I got really scared and began to cry. I knew I had done something wrong, but I was not sure what.

My dad found the store manager. I looked at him with tears in my eyes. The store manager looked at me, looked at my dad, looked at me and then back to my dad. My dad said, "My daughter has something to tell you."

With quite a few tears, I choked out my story of taking the candy and how I thought since it was on the floor it was okay to take. I said I was so sorry for taking it. The store manager was about to say something when my dad told him that I needed to learn this lesson now. The store manager said, "Well what would you like to do, Sir?"

He said, "My daughter will pay for it. I will give her the money, and she will pay for it out of her allowance when she gets home." The store manager thought that sounded fair. My dad gave him the money, and I took what was left of the candy home. Unfortunately, my dad made me throw away the candy and get the money I owed him.

On that day, I learned a huge lesson about integrity. I was young, but I had never been so ashamed of myself or so embarrassed. I remember the example vividly. I remember my dad had no qualms about taking me right up to the store manager and making me face what I had done. Integrity like that, is something I truly admire and when I was young I knew I wanted to aspire to that level of integrity. From that moment on, my dad was my hero. I knew I wanted to be like him. He had been in the military and he felt that his character had been solidified in the military. That is why I wanted to go to the Air Force Academy. I wanted the experiences the Air Force Academy offered to develop myself into a person with amazing character, a person like my Dad.

You need to find your why. During those rough days at the Academy, I thought about my dad and how much I wanted to be like him. So, I stayed. Now, my story was fairly long winded for an essay, but it could be shortened slightly for an interview and summarized for an essay. But consider the story from the point of view of an interviewer or admissions panel. They hear or read about students who want to attend a Service Academy because they are patriotic, want to fly, or be in the military. Many of the submissions sound the same.

Do you think anyone else will tell a story like mine? Probably not. In that story I offered up quite a bit of information about myself. I showed that I learned a great example about integrity and believe in character and patriotism. I also gave a very personalized example of why I wanted to attend the Air Force Academy. I differentiated myself from other students and gave those listening or reading interesting information about myself. That is what you need to do.

You need to personalize the why to you. The why is something very personal, very different, very specific, for each and every person. Finding your why gives you two things over everybody else. One, you know why you want to stay on those really bad days. Two, it gives whoever is interviewing you a very personal look into who you are. Remember to look at your answer from the point of view of your interviewer. They have heard hundreds stories about people who want to be patriotic or people who want to fly. The stories were very general and could be summarized in a sentence or two. Then the interviewer hears my story about my dad, me as a little kid, and stealing candy. If you were the interviewer, which story would you remember? Would you remember general stories about patriotism or would you remember a little girl crying and how her dad set such a great example for her?

You have to make the board see YOU if you want that appointment to the Air Force Academy. They need to see, you, not just a number, not just a file. They need to see you as an individual. To do that you need to think about your why. Then go a level deeper, and go a level deeper, and go down as many levels as you need until you find that story. Just keep asking yourself, why? What did you see? What event in your life seems to have set you down the path towards the Air Force Academy? What really affected and changed your life? Once you find it be specific and use as many details as you can to describe your why. Use your why to set you apart from everybody else.

Remember if you feel you need additional help or advice about your Air Force Academy application go to www.academypros.com. Professional Service Academy Consultants is dedicated to helping students through the application process while highlighting a student's unique characteristics that will make an Admissions Board take notice. We can be the "secret weapon" that guides the busy student and parents through the confusing and complex application process. Our consultants have worked in Service Academy Admission Offices and have the expertise to increase a student's chance of acceptance as well as answer any questions you might have. Also visit the Lauren Elliott Author Page on Amazon for additional titles.

Made in the USA
Columbia, SC
25 October 2020